PowerKids Readers:

The Bilingual Library of the United States of America™

Bilingual Edition
English/Spanish
Edición bilingüe

NORTH CAROLINA
CAROLINA DEL NORTE

DEAN GALIANO

TRADUCCIÓN AL ESPAÑOL: MARÍA CRISTINA BRUSCA

The Rosen Publishing Group's
PowerKids Press™ & **Editorial Buenas Letras**™
New York

Published in 2006 by The Rosen Publishing Group, Inc.
29 East 21st Street, New York, NY 10010

First Edition

Photo Credits: Cover © Chip Henderson/IndexStock Imagery, Inc.; p. 5 © Chuck Carlton/IndexStock Imagery, Inc.; p. 7 © 2002 Geoatlas; pp. 9, 19 © Will & Deni McIntyre/Corbis; p. 11 © Corbis; pp. 13, 15, 26, 31 (Madison, Angelou, Settlers) © Bettmann/Corbis; p. 17 © Museum of Flight/Corbis; pp. 21, 31 (Festival) courtesy of The Lexington Dispatch; p. 23 © Richard Cummins/Corbis; pp. 25, 30 (Capital) © Richard Cummins/Getty Images; p. 30 (Flowering Dogwood) © Farrell Grehan/Corbis; p. 30 (Cardinal) © Gary Carter/Corbis; p. 30 (The Tar Heel State) © Wally McNamee/Corbis; p. 30 (Longleaf Pine) © Raymond Gehman/Corbis; p. 30 (Emerald) © Philippe Eranian/Corbis; p. 31 (Jackson) © Stapleton Collection/Corbis; p. 31 (Monk) © Mosaic Images/Corbis; p. 31 (Gardner) © CinemaPhoto/Corbis; p. 31 (Earnhardt) © Duomo/Corbis; p. 31 (Tar) © Sarah Leen/National Geographic/Getty Images

Library of Congress Cataloging-in-Publication Data

Galiano, Dean.
North Carolina / Dean Galiano; traducción al español, María Cristina Brusca. —1st ed.
p. cm. — (The bilingual library of the United States of America) Includes bibliographical references and index.
ISBN 1-4042-3098-X (library binding)
1. North Carolina—Juvenile literature. I. Title. II. Series.
F254.3.G36 2006

975.6–dc22

Manufactured in the United States of America

Due to the changing nature of Internet links, Editorial Buenas Letras has developed an online list of Web sites related to the subject of this book. This site is updated regularly. Please use this link to access the list:

http://www.buenasletraslinks.com/ls/northcarolina

Contents

Contenido

Welcome to North Carolina

North Carolina is known as the Tar Heel State. Tar was once one of North Carolina's major goods. Tar was used to build ships.

Bienvenidos a Carolina del Norte

Carolina del Norte es conocido como el Estado Tacón de Alquitrán. El alquitrán fue uno de los productos más importantes de Carolina del Norte. El alquitrán se usaba en la construcción de barcos.

North Carolina Flag and State Seal

Bandera y escudo de Carolina del Norte

North Carolina Geography

North Carolina is in the eastern United States. North Carolina borders the states of Virginia, South Carolina, Georgia, and Tennessee. The Atlantic Ocean lies to the east.

Geografía de Carolina del Norte

Carolina del Norte está en el este de los Estados Unidos. Carolina del Norte linda con los estados de Virginia, Carolina del Sur, Georgia y Tennessee. El límite oriental del estado es el océano Atlántico.

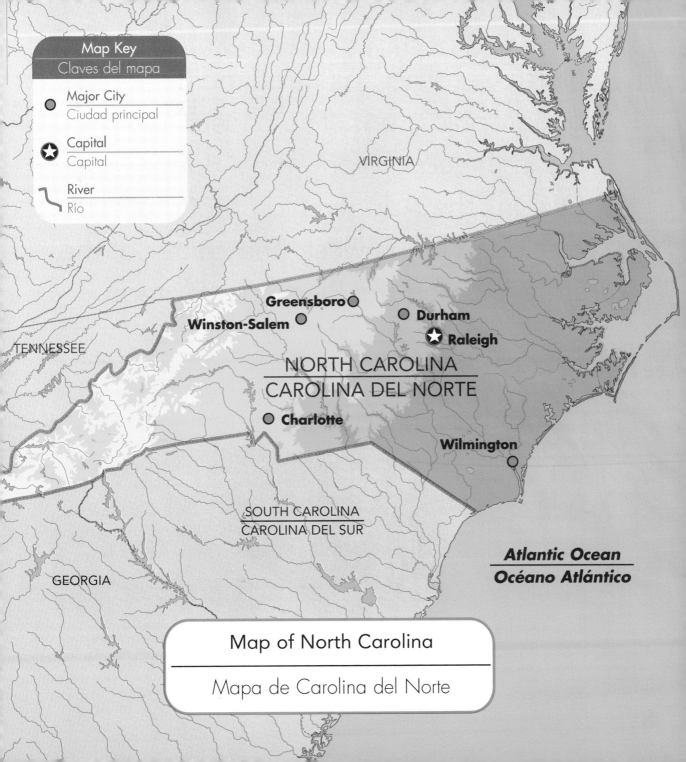

Map Key
Claves del mapa

Major City
Ciudad principal

Capital
Capital

River
Río

VIRGINIA

Greensboro
Winston-Salem
Durham
Raleigh

NORTH CAROLINA
CAROLINA DEL NORTE

TENNESSEE

Charlotte

Wilmington

SOUTH CAROLINA
CAROLINA DEL SUR

GEORGIA

Atlantic Ocean
Océano Atlántico

Map of North Carolina

Mapa de Carolina del Norte

North Carolina has three main geographic areas. The coastal plain lies in the east, along the Atlantic Ocean. The Appalachian Mountains are found in the west. The center of the state is called the Piedmont Plateau.

Carolina del Norte tiene tres regiones geográficas principales. La llanura costera se encuentra en el este y bordea el océano Atlántico. En el oeste se encuentran los montes Apalaches. El centro del estado se llama la meseta Piedmont.

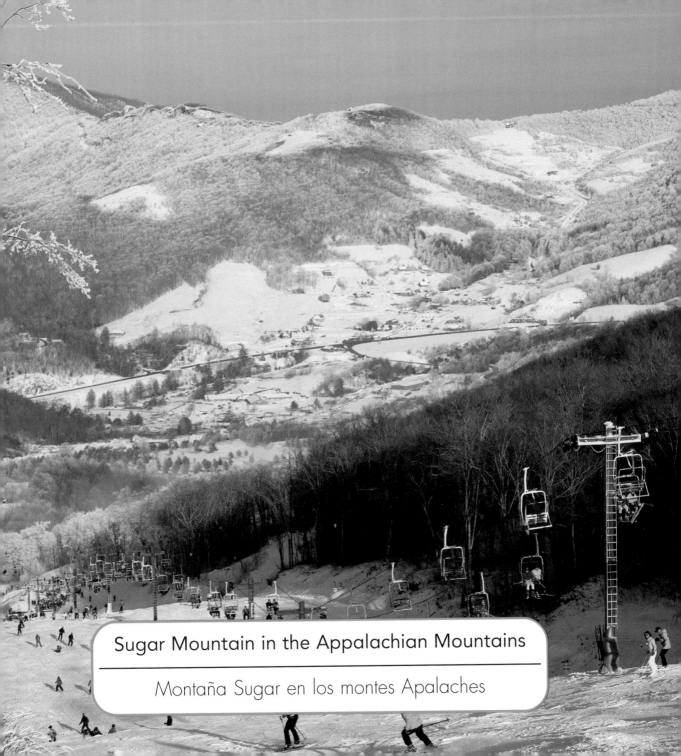

Sugar Mountain in the Appalachian Mountains

Montaña Sugar en los montes Apalaches

North Carolina History

Many Native American groups lived in North Carolina before Europeans arrived. The Cherokee lived in the Appalachian Mountains. The Algonquin lived along the coast.

Historia de Carolina del Norte

Muchas tribus nativoamericanas vivían en Carolina del Norte antes de la llegada de los europeos. Los Cheroquí vivían en los montes Apalaches. Los Algonquin habitaban la costa este.

Cherokee Boy and Girl

Jóvenes cheroquíes

In 1587, a group of 120 English settlers arrived at Roanoke Island to start a colony. Virginia Dare was born here. Virginia was the first baby born to English parents in North America. The colony mysteriously disappeared three years later.

En 1587, un grupo de 120 colonos ingleses llegó a la isla Roanoke para establecer una colonia. Allí nació Virginia Dare. Virginia fue el primer bebé de padres ingleses nacido en Norteamérica. La colonia desapareció misteriosamente tres años más tarde.

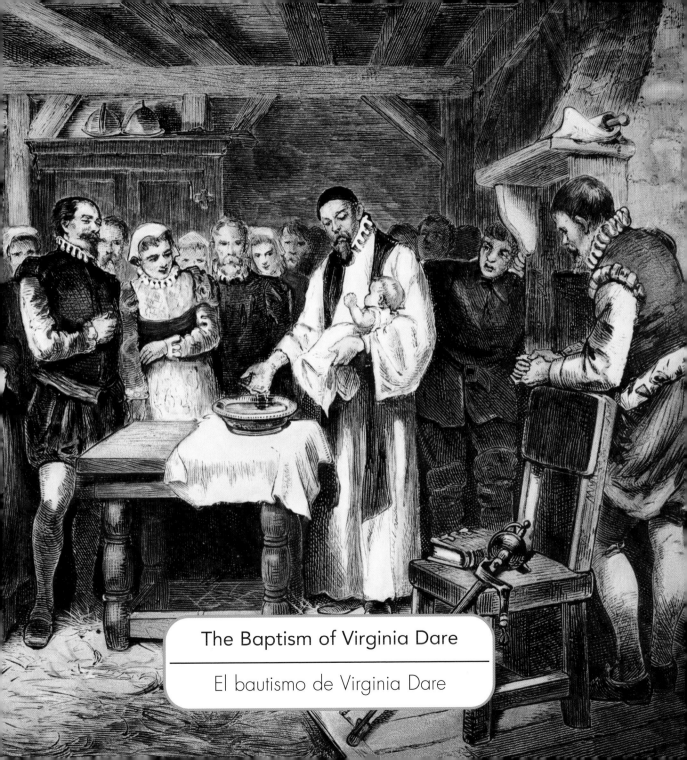

The Baptism of Virginia Dare

El bautismo de Virginia Dare

Dolley Payne Madison was born in North Carolina in 1768. She married James Madison, the fourth U.S. president. In 1814, the British army set fire to the White House. Dolley saved many treasures from the fire.

Dolley Payne Madison nació en Carolina del Norte en 1768. Payne se casó con James Madison, el cuarto presidente de E.U.A. En 1814, el ejército británico quemó la Casa Blanca. Dolley rescató muchos tesoros durante el incendio.

Dolley Payne Madison

On December 17, 1903, Orville Wright became the first person to fly an airplane. The flight took place at Kitty Hawk, North Carolina. It lasted 12 seconds and covered 120 feet (37 m).

Orville Wright fue la primera persona en volar en un avión, el 17 de diciembre de 1903. El vuelo tuvo lugar en Kitty Hawk, Carolina del Norte. El vuelo duró 12 segundos y atravesó una distancia de 120 pies (37 m).

Orville Wright and His Airplane, Named *Flyer*

Orville Wright y su avión, llamado *Flyer* (Volador)

Living in North Carolina

Eastern North Carolina has many sandy beaches. Many North Carolinians visit places like Emerald Isle, Duck, and Kitty Hawk. They enjoy swimming and fishing in the ocean.

La vida en Carolina del Norte

En la región oriental de Carolina del Norte hay muchas playas. Muchos norcarolinos visitan lugares como Emerald Isle, Duck y Kitty Hawk. Disfrutan de la natación y la pesca en el océano.

Cape Hatteras National Seashore
_____

Costa nacional Cabo Hatteras

In Lexington, North Carolina, October is called Barbecue Month. Many North Carolinians enjoy the Barbecue Festival. During the festival people take part in the cycling event called the Parade of Pigs.

En Lexington, Carolina del Norte, octubre es conocido como el Mes de la Barbacoa. Muchos norcarolinos disfrutan del Festival de la Barbacoa. Durante el festival la gente participa en un evento ciclístico llamado Desfile de los Cerdos.

Parade of Pigs

Desfile de los Cerdos

North Carolina Today

More than 8 million people live in North Carolina. Charlotte is the state's largest city. Charlotte is home to many large businesses.

Carolina del Norte, hoy

Más de 8 millones de personas viven en Carolina del Norte. Charlotte es la ciudad más grande del estado. Charlotte es la sede de muchas grandes empresas.

A View of the Charlotte Skyline

Una vista de los edificios en Charlotte

Charlotte, Raleigh, Greensboro, Durham, and Winston-Salem are important cities in North Carolina. Raleigh is the capital of North Carolina.

Charlotte, Raleigh, Greensboro, Durham y Winston-Salem son ciudades importantes de Carolina del Norte. Raleigh es la capital de Carolina del Norte.

State Capitol Building, Raleigh, North Carolina

Capitolio del estado en Raleigh, Carolina del Norte

Activity:
Let´s Draw Orville and Wilbur Wright's Airplane

Actividad:
Dibujemos el avión de Orville y Wilbur Wright

1

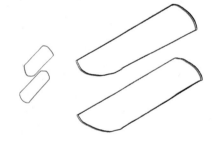

First draw the two shapes as shown for the airplane's wings. Add two smaller shapes for the tail. Note the placement of the small shapes.

Primero traza las 2 formas grandes para dibujar las alas del avión. Luego traza 2 formas más pequeñas para la cola del avión. Fíjate en la ubicación de éstas formas.

2

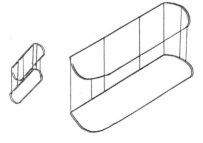

Connect the shapes with 13 vertical lines.

Conecta las formas con 13 líneas verticales.

3

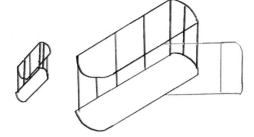

Draw a rounded rectangle to the right of the wings. Connect the rectangle to the wings with two horizontal lines.

Dibuja un rectángulo con las puntas redondeadas a la derecha de las alas. Conecta este rectángulo a las alas trazando 2 líneas horizontales.

4

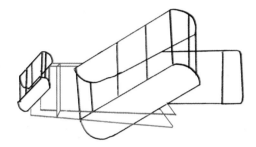

Draw the bars that connect the wings to the tail. Study the lines before you start.

Traza líneas rectas para dibujar las barras que conectan las alas a la cola. Observa bien las líneas antes de comenzar.

5

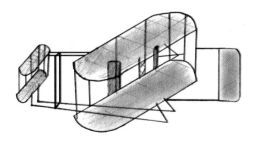

Add three shapes between the wings. Shade the airplane and you are done!

Agrega 3 formas rectangulares entre las alas. Sombrea el avión, ¡y habrás terminado!

Timeline

Sir Walter Raleigh sends colonists to Roanoke Island to create the New World's first English colony.

Nathaniel Bats becomes the first European man to settle permanently in North Carolina.

North Carolina becomes the twelfth state of the Union.

The University of North Carolina is founded. It is the nation's first state university.

Andrew Jackson, born in North Carolina, becomes the seventh U.S. president.

North Carolina leaves the United States to join the Confederacy in the American Civil War.

The Wright brothers make the world's first airplane flight at Kitty Hawk.

The Raleigh-Durham area is ranked the best place to live in the United States.

Cronología

1584
Sir Walter Raleigh envía colonos a la Isla Roanoke para crear la primera colonia inglesa en el Nuevo Mundo.

1655
Nathaniel Bats es el primer europeo en establecerse permanentemente en Carolina del Norte.

1789
Carolina del Norte se convierte en el estado número doce de la Unión.

1795
Se funda la Universidad de Carolina del Norte. Ésta es la primera universidad estatal del país.

1828
Andrew Jackson, nativo de Carolina del Norte, llega a ser el séptimo presidente de E.U.A.

1861
Carolina del Norte abandona a los Estados Unidos y se une a las fuerzas de la Confederación en la Guerra Civil.

1903
Los hermanos Wright realizan el primer vuelo mundial en avión, en Kitty Hawk.

1994
El área Raleigh-Durham es clasificada como el mejor lugar para vivir de los Estados Unidos.

North Carolina Events/
Eventos en Carolina del Norte

April
Apple Chill Street Fair in Chapel Hill

May
Greater Hickory Smoke Barbeque Fest in Hickory MerleFest in Wilkesboro

June-July
Appalachian Summer Festival in Boone

July
Bele Chere Festival in Asheville

August
Winterville Watermelon Festival in Winterville

September
Lake Lure Festival of the Arts in Lake Lure

October
North Carolina State Fair in Raleigh Barbecue Month in Lexington

December
Wake Forest Christmas Parade in Wake Forest

Abril
Feria callejera Apple Chill, en Chapel Hill

Mayo
Fiesta Greater Hickory Smoke y Hickory Merlefest, en Wilkesboro

Junio-julio
Festival de verano apalache, en Boone

Julio
Festival Bele Chere, en Asheville

Agosto
Festival de la sandía de Winterville, en Winterville

Septiembre
Festival de las Artes de Lake Lure, en Lake Lure

Octubre
Feria del estado de Carolina del Norte, en Raleigh
Mes de la Barbacoa, en Lexington

Diciembre
Desfile de Navidad de Wake Forest, en Wake Forest

North Carolina Facts/
Datos sobre Carolina del Norte

<u>Population</u> 8.4 million		<u>Población</u> 8.4 millones
<u>Capital</u> Raleigh		<u>Capital</u> Raleigh
<u>State Motto</u> To be rather than to seem		<u>Lema del estado</u> Ser antes que parecer
<u>State Flower</u> Flowering dogwood		<u>Flor del estado</u> Dogwood
<u>State Bird</u> Cardinal		<u>Ave del estado</u> Cardenal
<u>State Nickname</u> The Tar Heel State		<u>Mote del estado</u> Estado Tacón de Alquitrán
<u>State Tree</u> Longleaf pine		<u>Árbol del estado</u> Pino de aguja larga
<u>State Song</u> "The Old North State"		<u>Canción del estado</u> "El Estado del Viejo Norte"
<u>State Gemstone</u> Emerald		<u>Piedra preciosa</u> Esmeralda

Famous North Carolinians/
Norcarolinos famosos

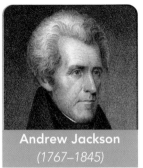

Andrew Jackson
(1767–1845)

U.S. president
Presidente de E.U.A.

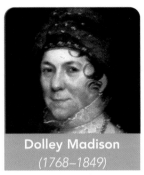

Dolley Madison
(1768–1849)

First Lady
Primera dama

Thelonious Monk
(1917–1982)

Musician/Composer
Músico/Compositor

Ava Gardner
(1922–1990)

Actress
Actriz

Maya Angelou
(1928–   )

Author
Escritora

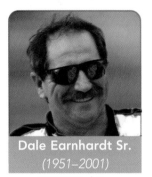

Dale Earnhardt Sr.
(1951–2001)

NASCAR driver
Piloto de NASCAR

Words to Know/Palabras que debes saber

border
frontera

festival
festival

settlers
colonos

tar
alquitrán

Here are more books to read about North Carolina:
Otros libros que puedes leer sobre Carolina del Norte:

In English/En inglés:

North Carolina
This Land is Your Land
by Heinrichs, Ann
Compass Point Books, 2003

Uniquely North Carolina
by McClellan, Adam and
Wilson, Martin
Heinemann Library, 2004

Words in English: 317

Palabras en español: 371

Index

Índice